FOUNTAIN OF HOPE

Ignatian Wisdom to Guide the
Work of Justice in a Turbulent World

© Anamchara Books, 2025

All rights reserved. No part of this publication may be reproduced or transmitted for commercial purposes, except for brief quotations, without written permission of the publisher. Churches and other noncommercial interests may reproduce portions of this book without the express written permission of Anamchara Books, provided that the text does not exceed 500 words or 5 percent of the entire book, whichever is less, and that the text is not material quoted from another publisher. When reproducing text from this book, include the following credit line: "From *Fountain of Hope: Ignatian Wisdom for the Work of Justice in a Turbulent World*, published by Anamchara Books. Used by permission."

Cover design: Ellyn Rae Sanna. Interior design: Micaela Grace. Editor: Ellyn Sanna.

ANAMCHARA BOOKS
Vestal, New York 13850
www.AnamcharaBooks.com

Print ISBN: 978-1-62524-925-8
eBook ISBN: 978-1-62524-926-5

FOUNTAIN OF HOPE

Ignatian Wisdom
to Guide the Work
of Justice in a
Turbulent World

PATRICK SAINT-JEAN SJ

INTRODUCTION

In 2020, while I was teaching at Creighton University in Omaha, I created a course on positive psychology and Ignatian spirituality as they apply to the current world. I was always happy to wake up every Monday and Wednesday morning, knowing soon I would join twelve upper-class psychology students to talk about race, racism, discernment, prayer, the state of the human heart, and more. While I was with them, I nearly forgot about the frightening realities outside our classroom.

In one session, we discussed our world's need for a psychology and spirituality of hope. In the midst of an ongoing pandemic of disease, racial violence, and other life-threatening crises, only hope, we realized, would give us the courage to keep going.

One student raised her hand. "But what is hope? Really? If you google the word, you get a definition—but nothing that tells you how to find hope. How to live it."

Another student spoke up. "You guys—you Jesuits—have what we need," he said, speaking directly to me. "Ignatian spirituality is all about giving hope to people who find themselves in holes they can't get out of. Ignatius knew all about crises, and he also knew about hope—and he had some really practical advice. You Jesuits have to step in. This is something you could do for us all.

For a moment, I was speechless. I realized then that the world's hopelessness directly challenges both my spiritual and professional commitments. Both Ignatian spirituality and psychology shed a light on the possibility that still exists in the world; hope is what springs from this possibility. I asked myself: *Can I take what I know—as a psychologist and a Jesuit—and offer it as a gift to others?* This book is the answer to that question.

In the years, however, between that classroom discussion and the writing of this book, I found myself navigating a desert of hopelessness, my compass of possibility utterly deactivated. War rages in the Middle East, Ukraine, Russia, and several countries in my ancestral continent, as well as gang warfare in the country where I was born. Natural disasters challenge the resources of local authorities. Violence and the ongoing effects of climate change have displaced hundreds of thousands of people around the world, and now other countries refuse to accept them. People lack adequate resources for medical care, education, and employment. What once looked like opportunities seem to have shriveled on the vine, blighted by new governmental policies and a growing tide of factionalism.

In the midst of so many crises, I didn't know how to recover what I considered to be the normal flow of life. As Shakespeare's Hamlet said, "Time is out of joint."

In times like these, when we perceive so much danger in our surrounding world, we extrapolate our fear into the future. We begin to believe the future holds no new possibilities. This is what it means to lose hope.

Hopelessness leads to anxiety. We long for the past, when we thought we were more secure, when life seemed to make more sense—but that longing only makes things worse, for we cannot regain what has been lost. By contrast, the present time seems strange and dissonant, unfamiliar and terrifying. If we can find no hope for the future to encourage us and lead us forward, our anxiety may turn to depression.

This depressed, anxious, despairing condition cripples human imagination. We lose our capacity to imagine a radically better world, a world of justice, interconnection, and cooperation. Everywhere we look, we see war, hate, fear of one another, ecological destruction, and various forms of inequality—racism, ageism, sexism, transphobia, homophobia, and more. We cannot imagine that anything good will come next. We act as though we have reached the end of a hideously tragic novel. Nothing to do now but close the book and—what? We have no answers.

Those of us who call ourselves Christians—followers of Jesus, the God-Human—may turn to scripture. Some of us find there a roadmap for hope. Meanwhile, though, others use scripture to justify injustice, leaving us with what look like two very different forms of Christianity. Those of us who long for justice may become cynical about our faith. We lose hope in hope itself.

But in that classroom in 2020, the students challenged me to find a different way. They made me remember what my grandmother always called me: *a man of hope.*

She told me she called me this because of something that happened when I was a baby in Haiti. My father had been involved in politics, and one night the opposition party came to our home and set fire to our house. At three in the morning, my mother woke me and my two older siblings; as we ran for our lives through the smoke, she murmured over and over, "With Christ, life is possible. There is always hope."

Despite that early experience, in the years since then, I've had my share of hopelessness. Always, though, my grandmother's title for me drew me forward, reminding me to seek new possibilities. I have done my best to express that hope in all my books.

Lately, though, I have not felt much like a man of hope. When my Ignatian family called on me to write a book about hope, I tried to run away. I was discouraged, spiritually drained. In this frame of mind, how could I write a book that would encourage other people?

When I confessed my dilemma to my spiritual director, he suggested I read some of the letters written by Ignatius of Loyola. Feeling dry and uninspired, I nevertheless began to read—and discovered in these letters a fountain of hope.

Ignatius did not often use the word *hope* in his letters, and yet he always saw beyond whatever dilemma was presented to him (which is truly the essence of hope). He had practical suggestions that showed his readers alternatives to their despair and frustrations. He wrote often to people mired in destructive conflict, and always, he offered practical suggestions for dealing more effectively, more lovingly with those we think of as enemies. No problem was too small or too big for his faith in God and his astute psychological insights.

I was refreshed and encouraged. Filled with inspiration (which is itself a form of hope), I called my editor at Anamchara Books, Ellyn Sanna. She immediately agreed: Yes, this was a book we needed to create.

As a clinical psychologist, I was impressed by Ignatius's shrewd understanding of human nature. The sixteenth-century crises he addressed in his letters were not so different from the twenty-first century's, and again and again, he spoke directly to my own situation. If you are seeking hope in a hopeless world, I believe he will also speak to you.

As Friedrich Hölderlin reminds us, "Where the danger is, also grows the saving power." Hölderlin, the eighteenth- and early-nineteenth-century poet and philosopher, faced unspeakable loss, isolation, and rejection in his lifetime; as a result, he was familiar with both hope and hopelessness. When we lose "faith in anything great," he wrote, we "are doomed, then, doomed to perish unless that faith returns, like a comet from unknown skies." Like Ignatius, Hölderlin found his comet (though I'm sure his vision of it must have often flickered); he found hope and faith, even in the depths of despair.

How and why did both Ignatius and Hölderlin have reason to hope? First and foremost, they found hope in the resurrection of Christ. Jesus shows us that even death is not the end of the story. He demonstrates that what looks like an ending can actually be a new beginning.

This is no easy, pain-free answer to all our problems. Jesus suffered agony; with all his human senses, he experienced the violation and destruction of his body. When we commit ourselves to the work of Jesus, building the Realm of Heaven here on Earth, we too may be called on to suffer.

We cannot avoid the reality that this present period of history is a time of reckoning. I'm reminded of the words Jesus spoke to his friend Peter: "The adversary insists on sifting you like wheat (Luke 22:31). The sifting process is a painful one. It shakes our reality in order to separate out what is valuable from what is not. It demands that we release our claim to the "chaff" that pollutes that which is wholesome and nurturing.

In times of crisis like the one we face today, the sifting process is particularly painful and frightening. If we are people with enough privilege, we might think we can retreat into the safe bunkers of our individual homes, refusing to see the terror and destruction that's going on outside. But there is no true way to avoid the demands this crisis puts on us as followers of Christ. We can say no to this challenge or we can say yes, but either way, we will be sifted. And we are not merely being sifted as individuals; our entire world is being tested.

This sifting process is a form of examination. Ignatius was big on self-examination (as you'll see when you read this book). He thought it should be a daily practice, essential to both our inner and outer lives. At the back of this book, you'll find a form of the Examen, Ignatius's favorite spiritual tool for self-awareness, one he himself used many times throughout each day.

As a psychologist, I am always struck by Ignatius's accurate insights into the value of courageous, objective self-examination. As he addresses the various problems his correspondents face, he has a nearly uncanny way of seeing past appearances to the true heart of each challenge. Again and again, he points the reader to look within. This steady self-awareness challenges our entire lives: our way of praying, thinking, seeing, acting, and interacting.

Today's circumstances force us to move in one direction or another. Whichever way we choose, we will be changed. We will either grow closer to Christ, actively embodying his work in our lives—or we will lose sight of who Jesus really is, and our hearts will grow cold.

Lately, every day brings new crises. New terrors pile on top of older ones faster than we can keep up. We grow exhausted from the sheer volume and speed of the destruction around us. But we have another option: We can allow the constant state of crisis to push us forward, one small, unsteady step at a time.

You've probably seen memes that say the Chinese character for the word *crisis* combines the meanings *danger* and *opportunity.* Regardless of how accurate this is when it comes to the Chinese language, the trope contains real truth; both aspects of a crisis are very real.

Our response to danger is fear, a primal emotion that from an evolutionary perspective contributes to the survival of many creatures. In modern life, however, fear is not always as useful as it once was as a basic survival mechanism. We cannot simply run from the wild beast that wants to eat us, nor can we turn and clobber it with a stick, not when the "wild beast" is a prevailing atmosphere of hatred.

Since the ancient fight-or-flight reaction does us no good, we have found a third option: *freeze.* It's not a very useful response, though. If our ancestors had all stood frozen whenever they encountered a threat to their safety, most of us today would not exist. If my mother had been paralyzed with fear when our house burst into flames, I would have died as a baby, along with the rest of my family.

Focusing only on the *danger* aspect of our present crisis smothers our powers of imagination. We perceive only limited options:

- We can try to flee (though there is no way to escape when our very planet is at risk).

- We freeze, terrified to act, so immobilized that we do nothing to counter the wave of destruction sweeping over our world—and so we are doomed.

- Or we fight tooth and nail against what we perceive to be the sources of danger.

You might think that as a Jesuit and a man of hope, I'm about to ask you to join me in the battle against the dangers that confront us. You may expect the Ignatian wisdom in this book to guide our fight against misguided leaders and fellow citizens. But that's not the direction I'm going, and it's not the direction Ignatian went.

Instead, Ignatius calls us to focus on *opportunities*. Instead of fighting, we reach out our hands. Instead of tearing each other down, we do our best to build each other up. Instead of hating our enemies, we learn to love them, as Jesus told us to do. We begin to see them as hurting human beings in desperate need of Christ's healing. We encourage and challenge each other, as my students did me in that classroom back in 2020. We find opportunities to transform society and become better human beings.

In his letters, Ignatius offers us a syllabus of hope. He gives practical advice for facing the never-ending difficulties that hinder God's work of justice, from our stubborn opponents to our own sexual temptations. His counsel is as insightful for the trivial, tedious hindrances as it is for the larger, more dangerous challenges. He shows us how to keep moving, despite weariness, illness, frustration, opposition, confusion, or lack of resources.

Hope always implies motion. It points forward, never behind us or to our present location. It calls us to *move*. To take action. To be alert for new possibilities. It is an internal leitmotiv, singing constantly at the back of our consciousness, like my mother's whispered words as she left behind a burning house. Hope gives us courage. It renews our confidence that the future holds new possibilities.

As Meg Llewellyn wrote in another Anamchara book, *Persistent Resistance,* the original root meaning of the word *hope* was "confidence in the future." Llewellyn goes on to stress that this confidence is not the same as optimism; it's not the comforting certainty that everything's going to turn out okay. Instead, we express our confidence in the future, she writes, not with our emotions but by doing whatever we can to build a brighter tomorrow, even when our emotions may seek to keep us mired in the past.

"Hope is a frame of mind," Llewellyn continues, ". . . that doesn't waste time looking over its shoulder at the past, and it doesn't worry about what could have been—but at the same time, it doesn't insist on its own way. It is open to the mystery of grace. It's willing to be surprised." She reminds us that we cannot seek to change the world if we refuse to be transformed ourselves along the way.

Ignatius is someone who was transformed by hope. When a cannonball crippled him during battle, his injury ended his career as a soldier—but at the same time, it was a new beginning. In his writings, we see his progress from an immature young man focused on military force, to the wise saint who could offer compassion and acceptance to everyone.

Today, Ignatius still invites us to create something new in our world. He reminds us that we are called to be Christ's co-workers in justice. We are co-creators with the Creator who never stops bringing new possibilities into being. In the many letters he wrote, Ignatius left us a legacy of hope.

This book is drawn from those letters. For each of the seventy-six meditations that follow, I pulled together a paragraph or two drawn directly from Ignatius's writing, followed by a short prayer. Sometimes I used his original wording; other times, I paraphrased and expanded, putting his thoughts into simple modern language that speaks specifically to the work of justice. At the back of the book, you'll find notes that indicate something about the particular circumstances Ignatius was addressing in each of his original letters.

Ignatius reminds us that the work of justice will always require patience: patience with ourselves, with one another, and with the world around us. Patience even with God! Ignatius asks that we see past the current external appearances and imagine a different reality. This act of imagination—always seeking to find the possibilities that can emerge from even the most terrible circumstances—empowers us to be people of hope.

This book is my invitation to you to join Ignatius of Loyola—and me—in an ongoing work: building the Realm of Heaven in our own homes, communities, nations, and planet. Ignatius's wisdom shows us how to move from the virtual to the real, from abstract to concrete, and from fantasy to reality. Ultimately, of course, only the original Creator of hope can help us as we work together with Christ.

I desperately needed the fountain of hope Ignatius opened for me in his letters. I suspect you do too. I hope you, like me, will be refreshed and encouraged, empowered to find Divine potential in every crisis. Together, let's plant the seeds that will grow into a flourishing garden, one that's constantly watered from a fountain of hope.

And, as the Cuban poet Alexi Valdes writes, may God make us all what "he had dreamed we would be."

— Patrick Saint-Jean SJ
January 21, 2025

*Hope is an embrace
of the unknown and the unknowable.*

—Rebecca Solnit, *Hope in the Dark*

Optimism disappoints, but hope does not.

—Pope Francis

*This world's not going to change
unless we're willing to change ourselves.*

—Rigoberta Menchú

*Practice goodness. Demand justice.
Give guidance to those who lean toward violence.
Be an advocate for vulnerable children and women.*

—Isaiah 1:17

The Body of Christ rejoices in you.

The work you do for Heaven's realm spreads like fragrance, giving encouragement and inspiration to people you may have never met. The generous Creator opened a fountain within your heart, and from it flows hope and truth. The Supreme Goodness is always eager to share Divine hope, always working to help you grow.

You need only be a vessel that's empty of ego, ready to receive grace—and ready also to cooperate diligently and sincerely with the work of God's love.

Here I am, Life-Giver.

Use me to do your work.

We are called to excellence, not mediocrity.

You are buoyed up and held steady by unconditional love—but at the same time, much is expected of you. Don't look at someone else and think, *Well, I'm doing better than that person so I must be doing okay.* And don't tell yourself, *At least I'm not as bad as* that *person.*

God's expectations are unique to each of us, so don't be distracted by comparisons. Don't settle for being anything but the best you can be, the person God is calling you to be, doing the work God created you to do: to give glory and honor to the Holy One; to become spiritually whole; and to help others and bring new hope into the world.

Yes, it's true that we all have this call—and yet it is not a call that goes out *in general.* Each of us is called to do this work within *specific* circumstances, among *particular* people, in our own unique ways. We need God's help to live out our call with courage, hope, and diligence, never settling for mediocrity.

I pray, All-Maker,

for the spiritual, emotional,

and physical energy I need

to do the work

to which you've called me,

to the best of my ability.

3

**Engage your drive
for excellence
with the work you do for God.**

No sports fan should show more enthusiasm for their team than you do for Heaven's work. No athlete or musician should have more dedication and self-discipline than you do. No soldier should demonstrate greater courage in battle than you do in your work for God's realm. If this world's activities can inspire such enthusiasm and commitment, how much more should Heaven's work fill us with the vital energy we need.

Encourage yourself by paying attention to individuals who are actively and effectively serving God. Learn from their example. Grow in hope.

*May I be enthusiastic

and hopeful, Holy One,

as I work with you

to build a better world.*

4

Passion empowers; apathy weakens.

A bow that's strung too tight easily snaps—but a slack string is just as ineffective. Be fervent and wholehearted in your commitment to learning, loving action, and hope. Your enthusiasm empowers your actions, while listlessness weakens them. As scripture tells us, "The lazy person's soul craves nothing and gets nothing, but the soul of the person who is decisive and determined will be rich and fulfilled" (Prov. 13:4). This holds true for both your interior and your exterior work.

Laziness and apathy never bring peace of mind, satisfaction, or excellence; they certainly don't engender hope! Instead, they breed uneasiness, for they hold us back from the very things that would help us achieve self-awareness and growth. Meanwhile, a passionate commitment to God yields contentment and achievement in this world, as well as spiritual well-being for eternity.

Energize me, Holy One,

with love's power,

that I may work with you

more effectively.

5

God enriches us and never impoverishes.

Employees do their work because they are paid to do so; no one expects them to work without wages. God also rewards us for our work. Divinity does not require us to be miserable and empty-hearted.

What is the Divine wage that's given to you as an individual? It's everything you are. It's every blessing you receive day by day, including the most ordinary ones like food and shelter, as well as your body's abilities (respiration, digestion, sight, hearing, and so on).

But your wages are still greater than that; they are wealth beyond your ability to see in this life. The Holy One shares with you all the treasures of Divine happiness and hope, and then God goes even further, allowing you to participate in the very essence and nature of Divinity. God gives you the entire universe, both that which you can see and that which you cannot.

And finally, Jesus himself is the wage all humans receive. In Jesus, Divinity became a part of the human family. He became poor that we might be rich, and now, he is both our support and our companion.

Thank you, Creator,

that you give me life—

and so much more.

May I take delight in all your gifts,

and may my joy empower me

with hope.

6

We are called to be instruments of Divine love and justice.

Although our faith may be a private matter, the times we are living in require that we work actively and obviously for the Realm of Heaven. Look around you. See how often people have forgotten the real teachings of Jesus. Notice how our society ignores his example. Meanwhile, human beings—each one an image of the Trinity and capable of experiencing a far different reality—are surrounded by ignorance, tormented by the storms of desire and meaningless fear.

Given the reality of today's world, it makes sense for us to do all we can to be effective instruments of Divine hope. When we see others fall short of Jesus' teachings, that's a call for us to do more.

Don't be distracted by being judgmental, condemning others' failures. Focus simply on being the best tool in God's hand that you possibly can, a powerful implement of Divine love and truth.

*In the words attributed
to Saint Francis, I ask,
Life-Giver, that I be
an instrument of your peace.
Where there is hatred,
let me bring love.
Where there is discord,
let me bring unity.
Where there is error,
let me bring truth.
Where there is doubt,
let me bring faith.
Where there is despair,
let me bring hope.
Where there is sadness,
let me bring joy.*

7

**Our emotions are meant
to be used in God's service—
but they are not meant to run the show.**

Indifference and apathy can be harmful to the work we do, but the opposite can be true as well: We can become *too* passionate, *too* emotional. Remember that Saint Paul tells us to serve God reasonably (Rom. 12:1).

Along the same lines, Saint Bernard writes that the enemy of our souls has no more powerful ruse for confusing us than by allowing our emotions to run away with us. Excited and uplifted with feeling, we assume we are demonstrating a deep and spiritual hope—when in reality, we have lost our connection to Divine love and truth. This self-deceit can work the other way too: overwhelmed with emotional pain, we may assume God has abandoned us, when in fact the One who gives us life is as close as our breath.

May my emotions empower me with your energy, Divine Goodness, rather than overpower me with ego-centered feelings.

All things in moderation—
even the work of justice.

"Nothing in excess," Plato advised, and this principle should be our guide even in matters pertaining to the work of God. When we fail to practice moderation, we may find our work accomplishes very little. Striving to achieve some particular goal, we are likely to encounter setbacks and inconveniences, particularly from our own bodies.

Remember, if a horse is ridden too hard, he may never finish the journey at all, and an overladen ship may sink to the bottom of the sea. God is not really served, not in the long run, when we push ourselves too hard. Furthermore, the Giver of Life wants us to take adequate care of our bodies, for they are the living temples of the Divine presence in the world; to mistreat them is equivalent to desecrating a church.

Curb my workaholic tendencies,

Beloved God, I pray.

9

Be good to yourself if you hope to do good for others.

Sometimes, when it comes to doing the work of justice, we're tempted to overload ourselves with things that really have no use. We might think we need a specific form of education, the support of a particular powerful person, or the cachet of a certain job title in order to work more effectively—when in reality, these things would only overburden us, overtire us, and distract us. We push our bodies too hard, trying to fit more into each day than twenty-four hours can actually hold. This attitude is like digging spurs into a horse that would be far more willing to run with just a tweak of the reins.

We need to practice discretion and discernment, so we can avoid going to extremes to the point we lose sight of our true goals. As Sirach tells us, we are no good to others, if we are not good to ourselves (14:5). He also says that God is pleased when we have compassion for own souls (30:24).

As I work for justice,

give me enough humility,

Friend Jesus,

to discern when to say yes

and when to say no.

10

Spiritual practices are not ends in themselves.

The disciplines of self-denial (such as fasting, praying instead of sleeping, or causing discomfort to our bodies in some other way) have helped many of God's followers achieve mastery over their selfish desires. These practices may be especially useful at the beginning of a person's spiritual journey.

But as we mature spiritually, we should not depend too much on these disciplines. We may become so focused on "mortifying our flesh" that we overlook the hopeful works of love to which God calls us. In this case, the disciplines we practice may even engender pride and arrogance in our souls, while at the same time, we weaken our bodies' ability to do the work of Heaven.

Remember, God did not call us to fast, practice chastity, or give away all our riches as ends in themselves. The only commandment Jesus gives us is this: that we love one another (John 15:12). Each thing we do should aid and support the love God extends to all people. Nothing should interfere with our participation in God's work of hope, reconciliation, and justice.

May I learn to curb

the selfish ego aspect

of my identity

in practical ways

that truly help other people.

11

Pressure and stress do not come from God.

Do you feel pressured to get more done *now*? Are you frustrated by all the steps you must take before you can act?

If so, keep in mind that God sees things from a perspective that's currently invisible to you. Think about a student who is studying to be a doctor; although she cannot yet practice medicine, she is already serving others with her dedication to her learning. Even if she dies while she's engaged in preparation, so that she never gets the chance to claim the name *doctor,* she will have still contributed to the work of Heaven. Since Divinity perceives time differently from humans, our intentions for the future have value in some way we cannot yet see.

In addition, we can offer ourselves to God each morning in service of others. With this offering as the foundation of our day, God will bring into our lives opportunities to help those around us. We do not need to do important public work to spread Divine hope.

All too aware of my failures

and imperfections,

Eternal One,

I'm often tempted to push myself

harder and harder.

Teach me to trust that life itself

channels your energy,

and make me alert

to each opportunity life brings

to do the work of hope.

As we grow spiritually, we help others grow as well.

Change in one thing inevitably brings about change in the things around it. This is true in both the physical world and the spiritual. Nothing stands alone. No new thing comes into being without the interaction of two or more other things. Life's interconnections are Divine channels of hope, growth, and generation.

Keep this truth in mind when circumstances hold you back from the work you long to do. God has put you in the place where you are right now. As you allow yourself to accept that, you will grow spiritually—and as you grow, the people around you will also change. Your life will filter into the world like a sweet fragrance, and your very being can be a catalyst for hope.

May I do my part

for the Realm of Heaven, Creator,

by committing myself

to my own ongoing growth.

13

Prayer takes many forms.

Do you feel guilty you don't have more time to spend in prayer? Prayer is essential to the work of Heaven, not optional—but you may be misunderstanding prayer's true purpose.

When the demands of life prevent you from spending hours in solitary contemplation or intercession, everything you do—household tasks, paperwork, conversations and other communications, anything at all!—can become a prayer as you offer it to God. This form of prayer is continuous, though it takes place in the background, and it will generate hope in your life and in the life of everyone you encounter. The Giver of Life honors your desire for Divine Love, no matter how it is expressed.

May each moment of my life

be a prayer to you,

Beloved God.

14

**Do not lose heart
Do not belittle yourself.
Others see and treasure God's gifts in you.**

The hopelessness or dryness of soul you seem to be experiencing may not be quite what you think. This feeling can come from a lack of confidence (in yourself and God)—and it can be cured by regaining that confidence. Remember, God is not as worried about this matter as you are.

God values that which gives substance and energy to the Divine work: patience, humility, the surrender of our egos. These are the qualities that allow us to serve God and our neighbor. Divinity grants us the other emotions, the ones we connect with faith and hope, as they are useful to us, but they are not essential to the spiritual life. These so-called "hopeful feelings" do not make us "good"—nor do they make us "bad" when they are absent.

Lover of my soul, may I take my emotional perceptions with a "grain of salt," so that they do not rule my thoughts and actions.

15

**No one
works alone.**

Neither you nor I can give anything we don't have. We cannot manufacture out of nothing some quality or skill that others need. This is why we need each other. As we are attentive to one another, caring for each other, we are each able to share what we have received from the Creator. Then, in turn, we too can receive what we lack from the gifts the Creator has given to others.

What others have to offer can make up for what you lack, just as you have much to offer that others may not have.

Thank you, Spirit,

that you don't expect me

to do the work alone.

Thank you we are all fueled

by your energy, as we do

the work of Heaven together.

May that reality give us hope!

16

Works of love take different forms.

When you confront someone who opposes your work, learn what you can from them. Assure them that you and others would be glad to help them in any way possible. By this, I don't mean you will help them tear down structures of justice; I mean you will do whatever you can to help their souls. All they have to do is accept your love (a love that comes from God).

One way to do this is by asking them questions. What occupies their time? What do they hope for? Offer your help and friendship. If they seem afraid or worried, encourage them to share their concerns.

Remind me, Creator,

that we are all one,

despite our differences.

May I work in love

to make this real

and illumine the world

with Divine hope.

17

Take care
when you communicate in writing.

Before you send any written communication, form a habit of looking it over first. Make any changes or corrections needed for clarity, to convey your meaning.

Honor the act of writing. Think of it as a way to spread Divine hope. Don't send anything that won't instruct and lift up the recipient.

Don't use busyness as an excuse for carelessness. Instead, let each written word be an expression of love, a conduit of hope. Be diligent and careful—and then your written communications will fuel your recipient's spirit with new energy.

May each word I write—

whether a text message,

an email, a comment on social

media, or something else—

console, enlighten,

and give new hope.

Self-examination sheds light on our paths.

Set aside time regularly for free and undisturbed though. Make yourself a magnifying lens through which Divine light can shine.

As you examine yourself, be calm. Be realistic. If you become aware of something in you that is weak, whether in your body or soul, be willing to consider setting aside your current responsibilities. Make your goal always to contribute both to the well-being of others and to a solid sense of Divinity at work in the world.

May my ego

never stand in the way

of bringing new hope

into the world.

19

Decision-making is a process that requires time.

When you need to discern a course of action, and you're not sure of the Divine will in these circumstances, ask if people close to you will pray for you for three days, seeking God's guidance for you. Meanwhile, on your part, set aside time during those three days to weigh your options. Consider each possibility objectively and carefully. Give this process your full attention.

Don't expect to see clearly quickly. Your perceptions may go up and down. Fear battles with hope, but in the end, if you are patient, your doubts will disappear. Wait until you have a sense of assurance and spiritual freedom. You will emerge with a greater sense of hope and resolve, ready now to work with God in a specific direction.

Give me patience, Life-Giver,

to wait for your clarity.

We follow God in community, but we discern the Divine plan for our lives as individuals.

What if you have undergone the process of discernment, reached a conclusion, and feel confident that you are proceeding in the right direction—only to find that people you respect have chosen a contrary route?

Don't worry about it! Continue on in the light the Life-Giver has shed in your life and don't concern yourself with other people's choices. It's entirely possible that while God pointed you in one direction, others received different but equally valid Divine direction. The Holy One will eventually bring these contrary forces together in a way that contributes to the Realm of Heaven.

May I go wherever you lead,

Source of all life, so that I shine

your hope into the world,

without judging

or condemning others

who have taken different routes.

21

Pay attention to your emotions, actions, and motivations.

Take care to put your love of God at the center of your thoughts and behaviors. Desire nothing so much as you desire the presence of the Holy One. Speak with the Divine in your heart, and consider these conversations more important than any others.

Then seek to love the people around you—your family, friends, colleagues, casual acquaintances, as well as people in the public arena—and set aside your own pleasures as necessary for the good of Heaven's realm.

Unselfish love is the only thing that will renew our world. It is the source of all our hope.

Show me, Beloved One,

how to be a conduit of your love.

22

Speak only when you truly have something to say.

Spoken words should always lead to greater understanding, whether your own or someone else's. God wants to use your conversations to build connections, break down walls of misunderstanding, and generate hope.

Avoid topics that do not nurture the soul. Don't spend much time discussing the news and worldly affairs, for these subjects do little to lead souls into the light. Be humble when you speak. Be kind. Don't gossip or complain.

May my words and conversations reflect your Light.

23

In your relationships, always follow Christ's example.

Don't seek to impress others with your cleverness, talent, or fashion sense. Don't be a know-it-all. Don't seek to outshine others with your eloquence.

Instead, study the way Christ interacted with others. He never tried to impress; he didn't care whether people admired or respected him. Motivated always by love, he chose humility—and with his words, expressions, and body language, he brought new hope to everyone he met.

Teach me to be humble, Jesus.

I want to speak, act,

think, and feel like you.

Remember: You are always in God's presence.

Whenever you consider a particular action, acknowledge to yourself that God is watching. Are you comfortable doing this thing, knowing the Divine Eye is upon you? Would you do this if you could see all Creation watching you?

Use your imagination to see past your physical perceptions. Whether you are aware or not, God and Creation are always present. Each action you take will have an effect on them both. Your every act can propagate hope.

Remind me daily, Life-Giver,

that you see each step I take.

Instead of focusing

on my selfish pleasures,

may I seek always to contribute

to the Realm of Heaven,

and the well-being of your Creation.

25

Care more about truth than you do power.

Don't insist you're right and others are wrong. Your stubbornness can get you into harmful arguments.

Instead, be patient with others, even when their arguments seem foolish or misinformed. Give reasons for your opinions, but not to prove you're right and everyone else is wrong. You don't need to have the upper hand in an argument to beget hope and spread the light of truth.

May I not be afraid

to speak truth, Holy One,

but may I do so humbly.

26

Make love your priority in all things.

Take care that nothing interferes with your love for your sisters and brothers. Pay attention and be firm with yourself. Turn away from any thought or action that gets in the way of love. Work hard to be tender and loving in all your interactions.

"This," said the One who is the Supreme Truth, "is how the people around you will know you are following me" (see John 13:35). This is how you will bring hope to a despairing world.

May others see you

in me, Jesus.

We all make mistakes!

If you realize you have done something harmful to yourself or others, don't worry that other people will think less of you. Don't become so discouraged you want to give up.

Instead, ask forgiveness of anyone you have hurt. Forget what others may think of you, and learn whatever you can from the experience.

And then, thank God that Divine light shines even through your mistakes. The Most Supreme One created you as you are, in both heart and body. You reach true humility when you realize God may have intended all along to work through the very fumblings and missteps of which you now feel so ashamed. Divine hope reaches far beyond our failures.

And if you see someone else making mistakes, remember you are just as likely to fail in similar or different ways. Simply pray for them.

Thank you, Beloved God,

that you are always

working for our good

and the good of all Creation,

even through our mistakes.

Honest conversations lead to greater self-awareness and deeper insights.

If you have a spiritual director or a close friend with whom you share your inner life, don't try to conceal from them your weaknesses and temptations. At the same time, be equally open and honest about thoughts and plans that please you.

Remember: Something painful may be the very thing your soul needs to grow, and something that seems pleasant may actually be harmful. As scripture says, "Even the adversary comes disguised as an angel of light" (2 Cor. 11:14).

Other people can see past our self-delusions. Honest and vulnerable conversations contribute to the self-awareness that opens your soul to the light of Divine hope.

Thank you, Infinite One,

for the people in my life

who see me more clearly

than I see myself.

29

Let justice and gentleness be your guide.

When you interact with others, don't go to extremes, seeking to impress them with a forced attitude of hopefulness. Don't be silly, constantly laughing and making jokes. On the other hand, don't trot out your sadness as though it were a prize horse.

As the apostle said, "Let your fairness and moderation be obvious to everyone" (Phil. 4:5). Let Divine justice guide your words and actions rather than your ego.

Remind me, All-Maker,

that my goal is not

to impress others

but rather to demonstrate

your gentleness.

30

Focus on God's call to you in the Now.

If you feel God calling you to a certain action, even a very small one, don't procrastinate. We often tell ourselves, "This isn't the right moment for this or that. Tomorrow or the next day will be better. I'll be able to achieve more if I wait." We think the future offers some perfection the present doesn't hold—but that is a lie.

God calls to you in the Now. Don't postpone your answer until some ideal future time. Hope grows from the seeds of the present moment, no matter how tiny those seeds may be.

Listen carefully to the Spirit. You cannot pull sprouts out of their seeds with your hands or stretch them into tall plants overnight. Instead, patiently nourish those seeds, moment by moment, until they grow tall enough for birds to come to perch (see Matt. 13:32).

Life-Giver,

lead me today to actions

that will build hope,

making the Realm of Heaven

visible in this world.

Serve and grow
within life's current circumstances.

We may feel committed to our calling from God—and yet our perceptions can become so clouded that we lose sight of the Divine direction for our lives. Restlessness, self-doubt, and false guilt can replace commitment, making us question ourselves. When our eyes shift from God's love to our own worries and doubts, hope withers.

This human tendency manifests in several ways. If God has called us to solitary lives spent in prayer, we may feel guilty we're not out there actively helping people—and the contrary may be true as well: Although God has called us to a busy life of active involvement, we long for a quieter, more contemplative lifestyle.

By focusing on what we *don't* have, though, we may miss out on the Divine gifts to us, right here, right now. As Saint Paul tells us, we can be content with whatever circumstances we encounter (Phil. 4:11), for God uses us in each and every one.

When I compare my life

to others' and find myself lacking,

remind me, Great Spirit,

that you have called me by name;

you lead me on a path

that's all my own.

You don't expect me to do

and be all things at the same time.

When it's time for a change,

you'll show me!

32

In all your interactions, be slow to speak and say little.

Have an open attitude. Be ready to listen more than you talk. Be patient, letting people speak for as long as they need to convey their thoughts. Then, give them the opportunity to ask questions. Answer succinctly, without rambling.

If you feel you need to speak a conflicting truth, be as brief as possible. When you're done, say goodbye promptly and politely. An aggressive or combative attitude never generates the hope the world needs!

Remember, this is not the interaction that will win or lose your cause; it is only a crumb in the ongoing work. Be faithful to that crumb, but do not seek to destroy your enemies with your words. Instead, you will do far more if you show them courtesy and kindness.

When the time comes for me

to speak truth to injustice,

may I do so

with goodwill and respect.

May I seek always

to listen and learn.

33

Understanding requires flexibility.

Get to know the people you're seeking to convince. Pay attention to their personalities and preferences—and then adapt yourself accordingly. If someone is chatty, cheerful, and lively, don't talk to them about justice with a serious face and a glum tone. On the other hand, if they are shy and reserved, follow their lead in that direction as well.

This kind of interpersonal flexibility contributes to understanding and helps remove the barriers between perspectives. Follow the example of the apostle Paul who "became all things to all people" (1 Cor. 9:22).

May I be adaptable, Holy One,

rather than rigid,

willing to change

my personal behaviors

rather than expecting others

to change for me.

34

Our different beliefs can lead to disagreements— but other factors may also be at play.

Be sensitive to other people's states of mind. Don't let personalities different from your own irritate you. If you're talking to someone you observe to be cranky and quarrelsome, take extra care with your words.

Always be aware that the other person may be unwell, in pain, and or dealing with some crisis of their own. These factors may also influence your interactions. Don't let a mere headache or an upset stomach hinder God's work.

*As I work on behalf

of hope and justice,

teach me, Living One,

to be sensitive

and patient with others.*

35

Enter through the other's door— but then lead them out through your own.

When you're trying to persuade someone to see the Divine path of justice and love, don't start out being negative and critical. Notice and affirm good qualities and behaviors. Don't focus on the points of disagreement. Practice being a good friend as your first goal, while you set aside your doctrinal or political differences.

This will allow you to enter the other person's life through *their* door, so to speak. You will have greater success if you focus on all you have in common rather than your desire to change their minds on certain points.

Then, when a genuine friendship has been established, you can share your own perspectives; in other words, you will reveal *your* door as the entryway into a different sort of life. You can be a friend who affirms the good in others, spreading hope and a sense of new possibilities, while still being true to your principles.

Instead, of seeing others

as enemies, Light-Giver,

teach me to see past our differences

and recognize

our common humanity.

36

**Lend a hand to people
who are sad or troubled,
just as you would
if they were in physical danger.**

Show kindness and compassion to anyone who is feeling discouraged or spiritually weak. Take time to talk with them. Do your best to share a sense of joy and hopefulness with them, both in your prayers and in your conversations.

Without lecturing or judging, seek to draw them away from their sadness and weakness. Your simple companionship will bring them hope.

*When I encounter people
who have fallen into
emotional or spiritual trouble,
remind me, Holy One,
that when I am sad,
you only want to comfort me;
you never condemn me
or punish me.
May I always seek
to be more like you.*

Guard your words.

Be careful when you are speaking, especially when you are working for peace and justice. Remember, everything you say can (and very often will) become public. Choose your words carefully, so that later you don't have reason to regret them.

Always remember—you represent the Realm of Heaven.

Spirit of Truth,

may my words shine

with your integrity

and bring hope

to those who hear them.

38

Some advice for situations of political conflict—

First, as always, focus on gratitude, even in these circumstances. Look for any benefits you have received from the situation, any kindness, any blessing, despite the anger and division around you. Take note of any good qualities, even in those who oppose your work, and express your thanks. When we complain rather than give thanks, we become vulnerable to the same harmful forces we seek to counteract. Gratitude gives birth to hope. It fixes our hearts and minds, giving them stability to resist the tides of evil. Through it all, the perfect grace and eternal love of Christ is our never-failing protection and help.

Second, remember you are not alone in this work. Though you may be geographically separated from others, together we each carry a share of the spiritual and physical labor. Together, we take up our spiritual weapons—having forever abandoned all physical weaponry—you in your place, while the rest of us work from other places, all of us persistent in daily prayer.

Finally, remember what is at stake here. Divine love always prevails, but the longer this situation continues, the more confusion it causes, and the more vulnerable people are put at risk. Do not lose your sense of urgency, even while you anchor yourself in the hope of Christ.

Keep me steadfast

in gratitude, Life-Giver,

always aware

that I am part of a greater work

that is ongoing

in both Heaven and on Earth.

39

Plan ahead for conversations that might drain you of hope.

Interacting with other people is a vital aspect of the work to which God has called us, but we need to always be alert, dependent on Divine grace. Some social interactions can also pull us down, causing us to lose our spiritual focus. As a result, we may even harm the people we seek to help.

Since we cannot simply run away when we find ourselves in a challenging conversation, it's a good idea to have a plan already in place. The more prepared we are, the more likely we are to stay on track.

Beloved One,

may my interactions with others

always be guided

by your light and hope,

your truth and justice.

May I not forget

that my storehouse of hope

can be quickly emptied

if I rely only on my own resources.

40

**Respect speaks more clearly
than a loud voice.**

You accomplish very little if you shout your opinions more loudly than anyone else, drowning out other voices. On the other hand, kindness and consideration do more for the Realm of Heaven than any words you might speak.

Always listen before you say anything. Giving the other person your full attention, you will better understand their meanings, desires, and feelings.

As you listen, you will learn to sense when to speak and when to be silent. Sometimes, silence can bring as much hope to others as any words we might utter!

Teach me, Jesus,

to listen to others

with both my heart

and my mind.

41

Respect
requires an open mind.

When you engage in discussions about controversial topics—and the situation requires that you speak rather than remain silent—set aside your attachment to your own opinions, so that you can honestly consider both sides of the question. Don't show favoritism based on personality or any other quality; treat everyone the same, doing your best not to offend anyone.

Don't name-drop, citing some authority to back up your point. Express yourself humbly and respectfully. Focus on the areas where you can agree. Instead of arguing about particular points of theology or politics, seek only to affirm the other person's identity and God's love. Our job is never to defeat or overpower but always to kindle hope with love.

Remind me, Light of All Life,

that love for others

is always far more important

than my opinions.

We need each other's insights.

We cannot work effectively for the Realm of Heaven without the support and insights our fellow workers offer us. No one can do everything alone.

Take time to talk with spiritual friends, sharing with them the events in your life and your plans for the future. Ask for feedback. Be open to hearing criticisms.

Our goal is not so much to become *better* people as to become more *loving* people. Love creates hope far more than any other quality we might possess.

Give me the humility I need,

Life-Giver,

to hear loving criticism—and then

apply it to my life.

43

Too much of a good thing can be harmful, to both body and soul.

Spiritual and physical health are both Divine gifts, yet at the same time, we each must play a part in ensuring our own health. Physical exercise can strengthen our bodies, and spiritual exercise has the same effect on our souls.

But that doesn't mean the same exercises are good for all people, nor should they be used at all times. A form of spiritual exercise that was once effective may no longer be when circumstances change, and what works for one person may not be helpful for another.

Here, as in all things, we must practice moderation, for just as too much physical exercise may overtax our bodies when we are ill, injured, or aging, so too much spiritual exercise may drain the hope from our hearts. God's desire is always that we be as strong and effective as we can be, not weakened by pushing ourselves too far.

Creator, you know my physical

and spiritual limitations

better than I do.

I ask for your wisdom to discern

where and when I need to do more—

and where and when

I need to do less.

44

**You need more prayer time
on some days
than you do on others.**

If we find fear and hopelessness overcoming our spiritual lives, we probably need to increase the frequency and length of our prayers. At other times, when our thoughts are filled with the Spirit's confidence, our only spiritual task is to open all the doors of the soul. In these circumstances, when we no longer need a spiritual tonic, we can safely reduce our prayer time. As we experience an ongoing vital relationship with the Creator, we can apply an energetic hope to the work of justice.

As our circumstances change, we must discern the amount and form of prayer that is most helpful for the situation. Just as no physician would advise amputation for a minor scratch on the finger, so should we be careful to use reason in applying the necessary treatment to our spiritual lives.

Keep in mind, though, that God holds and honors both depression and joy. If we feel spiritually weak or troubled, we do not hinder the Divine purpose in our lives, nor do we need to feel guilt or shame. By the same token, when our hope is strong and joyful, we have no cause for pride. So long as we sincerely seek to be part of the Divine plan, the Creator's work continues undiminished, in both weakness and strength, both anxiety and confidence.

May I be sensitive

to the condition of my soul,

Divine Friend,

giving it always

the care it needs most.

45

Your spiritual life can expand so that it absorbs the various elements of your daily life.

God may call some people to set aside their exterior roles and responsibilities to focus more completely on their inner lives—but most of us will continue to have various earthly affairs we need to attend to. Don't use the work of Heaven as an excuse to neglect your business or family responsibilities. Take time for conversations. Nurture your relationships. Make intentional learning a part of your life as well.

You don't need to be kneeling in a church to be in God's presence. In fact, your soul expands when you enjoy the Spirit in many different times and places. Do your best to always keep your inner self peaceful and quiet, always ready for whatever Divine Goodness wishes to work in you.

Thank you, Light-Giver,

for the many details of my life.

May I sense your Spirit in them all,

so that my hope in you

grows stronger.

46

Physical health influences spiritual acuity.

Many saints start their spiritual lives with fasting and various forms of abstinence, but as we grow spiritually, we learn the body is not our enemy. The inner being and the outer cannot be separated from one another, at least not while we are in the earthly realm. Both inner and outer identities are Divine gifts, and we are responsible for giving both the care they need.

Do not ignore or neglect your body, let alone damage it intentionally. Too much fasting, for example, can injure your digestive system and weaken your muscles. Your soul relies on your body's help and service. Love your flesh; don't treat it harshly. Do whatever you can to make it strong and healthy, so it can contribute to Heaven's work.

Remember that your brain is part of your physical being, and it also requires care and maintenance. When the mind is healthy in a healthy body, a sense of hope comes more easily. The entire self is better prepared to give greater service to the work of Divine justice.

I give you thanks, Life-Giver,

for my body—my flesh and bones,

my nerves and senses,

and the miracles of respiration,

digestion, thought.

Remind me to focus on all

the amazing things

my body can do,

rather than its flaws.

May I love my flesh,

knowing it is a wondrous aspect

of the identity you have given me.

47

Spiritual practices are not one-size-fits-all.

Many people fall into the error of believing God is pleased when we deny ourselves healthy pleasures. These people often try to prove their holiness with extreme actions that set them apart from the people around them. They seek an exterior form of holiness while they neglect their inner lives. They may also believe their specific religious practices are necessary for all people.

It's not our job to judge these people, but we can take care not to fall into the same confusion. The Spirit relates to us individually and privately, knowing what is most appropriate for each of us, given our circumstances and our level of maturity.

When we ask, the Spirit will always point us in the right direction. Meanwhile, we do our part in our relationship with One who gives us life by testing various spiritual methods to see which ones yield the most clarity. Which generate hope in our hearts? Which lead us most directly into the heavenly realm? Which help us feel the Divine Presence most clearly?

The answers to these questions are the standards to use as you commit to spiritual practices. You may learn new possibilities from other spiritual people, but do not concern yourself if ultimately you are led to a spiritual path that differs from theirs. Keep in mind that exterior, visible demonstrations of "holiness" are only useful to the extent they contribute to your spiritual well-being.

Remind me,

Holy One, not to compare

my spiritual life to others'.

And may I not judge people

who have chosen

another path than mine.

48

Some advice for doing good in the world—

When you commit yourself to work on behalf of Heaven's realm, your first and greatest asset may be something you'd never expect: a lack of confidence in your own powers. By this, I don't mean that you should undermine your work with self-doubt; I mean that you cultivate a realistic self-awareness. An objective realization of your flaws and weaknesses helps you avoid the arrogance and grandstanding that will truly undermine the good you seek to do. Trust that God will use you effectively, regardless of any weakness or failure on your part!

Add to this an ardent desire to be of service in creating a better world, a desire fueled by hope and love. This creates a two-fisted approach: Your desire keeps you focused, while at the same time, you leave everything in God's hands.

Finally, be alert for chances to act in love. When the Spirit leads you to these opportunities, make diligent and suitable use of them.

I ask, Beloved Spirit,

that you keep my passion

for justice burning—

and at the same time, remind me

that you will act through me,

even when I feel inadequate

for the work.

49

Your life—your being— has power.

We don't always need to be *doing* and *achieving*. Sometimes our most powerful influence comes from simply *being*. Without ever saying a word or accomplishing a single task, our lives can demonstrate hope.

Adapt yourself to the people around you, rather than expecting them to adapt to you. Do your best to bring cheer to those who are sad; notice when others are feeling challenged and find ways to be quietly helpful—but don't seek to appease and gratify people merely so they will think better of you. As much as you can, be friendly and respectful to people on all sides of the issue.

Everyone around you should be able to see your inner peace reflected in your exterior composure. Your very body language can convey hope to those who are watching.

Today, Life-Giver,

even if I get nothing "accomplished,"

may the essence of who I am

speak always of hope.

50

Don't try to do the work of justice all by yourself.

Before making decisions regarding the work, always take time to discuss options with your colleagues. Regularly seek input from other organizations and authorities.

Remember that when your own inner resources run short, you can draw on others' strengths. Don't allow yourself to become so busy that you forget your passion and energy need to be frequently renourished.

Don't be hasty to express your opinions. When asked for advice, take your time to think over the question before giving an answer. If necessary, ask for input from other people. Don't try to impress others by having all the answers off the top of your head! Let go of any urge to do this work independently to prove your own abilities.

May my selfish pride

not get in the way

of your work,

Spirit of Hope.

God is present in all things.

Given the demands of the work, you may find you have little time for prolonged meditation. In that case, simply seek God's presence in all things: your conversations, your travel, your walks, your meals. Divine power, hope, and essence are literally in everything you see, taste, hear, and understand, as well as all your actions.

This kind of meditation—finding God in all things—is easier than pondering abstract theological truths that require thought and attention. At the same time, this constant, simple practice prepares your spirit for both spiritual experiences and earthly work, when the time is right.

Part of this practice requires offering all your work and effort to God, so that everything you undertake becomes a vehicle of hope and love. Daily examine yourself to discern how consistently and sincerely you are practicing this form of spiritual devotion.

Eternal One,

teach me to see you

in every aspect of my life.

52

Criticism should build rather than tear down.

If you feel the need to correct someone who is working alongside you, consider these two questions: First, do you have the authority to give this person advice? (In other words, is it really any of your business?) And second, can you offer criticism with sincere love for the other person? If you can't meet these two criteria, it's better to keep quiet, because the other person will be unlikely to change.

If, however, after prayer and careful thought, you determine it is indeed appropriate for you to correct this person, talk to them gently and tactfully in private. Don't speak in anger or with a harsh tone; notice the other person's state of mind and adapt yourself accordingly. Even after you've done all that, though, don't be surprised if the person's behaviors remain the same. You have done what you could; leave the rest in God's hands. Our hope never depends on human actions.

If there's a problem within your organization, focus on improving the group's effectiveness as a whole, rather than casting blame on any single individual. In most cases, it's better to worry about our own imperfections, rather than criticizing others. The more we pay attention to someone else's flaws, the less aware we are of our own.

Only when Divine love has expanded our hearts sufficiently, can we speak truth to error as an expression of love.

Remind me, Jesus,

that I'll never remove

the speck in my friend's eye

when a plank obscures

my own vision! (Matt. 7:5)

53

Look after your physical health!

Confronted with so much work to be done for the cause of Divine justice, you may push yourself to do more and more, exceeding your body's abilities to keep up. Although your motivation is good—if, that is, you're sincerely seeking to work always on behalf of Heaven's realm—still, you are ultimately doing more harm than good if you ignore your body's demands. Bodies cannot continue indefinitely without proper care, and rather than advancing Divine hope, you may end up having to curtail or cease your activities because of illness.

If you have already driven your body to the breaking point, take some time off—even a few months—to heal and restore your physical well-being. See a doctor, and then follow her advice regarding your diet, the hours you sleep, and how you use the rest of your time. Meanwhile, leave the work in God's hands.

Teach me to listen to my body,

Creator.

May I honor its needs

and treat it with respect.

54

When doing the work of justice, we don't simply want more warm bodies; we want people who are there for the right reasons.

Encourage volunteers to participate in your work; this can be one of the best ways to teach others about what you are doing. Be careful, though, when recruiting new workers. They should be able to demonstrate both their passion and their commitment to the work—and they should be as willing to do small necessary tasks as they are to do larger, more dramatic ventures. You don't need people who are looking for attention and praise, who are seeking their own glorification by means of this work.

Create a structure to keep the work orderly. Tasks can then be delegated according to each person's abilities. Don't assign work to people who lack the maturity or experience to handle that particular task. Maintain a cooperative work atmosphere, where each person seeks to help one another, and no one tries to outshine the others.

Give us, Holy One,

practical wisdom

and keen business insight

as we seek together

to spread your hope.

55

Every community has many needs— but we can't meet them all!

It can be hard to decide how far to extend our efforts. This means we must take time to discern where to expand our work and where to limit it.

Find out what other work is already going on in your community; do your best to cooperate with them, so that you support and encourage each other's efforts.

When we share a common goal, it doesn't matter who does the work, so long as it gets done!

Thank you, Life-Giver,

that your body is large,

containing many parts.

May we all work together

to be the hands and feet,

mouths and minds

that make hope real.

56

**No work can be done
without the necessary resources—
and money is one of those necessities.**

Few things undermine hope so much as a lack of resources. Before all else then, make the work's finances a matter for ongoing prayer.

Don't neglect fundraising, seeking out organizations and individuals who may already have an interest in your area of work. Be friendly and courteous; allow the Holy One to speak through you, using your words. To avoid needing to return with your hand out again and again, suggest a fixed monthly or annual amount of support. Communicate your sense of confidence and commitment to the work, so that possible benefactors won't wonder if your organization will last long enough for their money to do any good.

Remember, you are asking on behalf of your efforts to build a more just world, not to promote your own interests. You should make this clear, so that no one thinks you're being greedy. When asking for necessary financial support for yourself individually (no one can live on air alone!), it may be best to have one of your colleagues do that on your behalf.

Don't hesitate to seek help and guidance from people who have more experience in fundraising than you do!

Beloved God,

when I am hesitant to ask

for the financial support we need,

remind me that I'm asking for you

and for those in need,

not myself.

57

The many details this work requires can be distracting—but that doesn't mean we should seek to excuse ourselves from work we find unsatisfying.

While paying the bills or mopping the floor, it's often hard to remember we are working in partnership with Divine Goodness to build a more just world. We may lose sight of the greater goal—or we may resent the menial and seemingly trivial work that takes up so much time.

A change of attitude, however, can shift our perceptions. When we accept distractions as aspects of our service (to God and others), when we even welcome them as moments bestowed on us by Divinity, then the ordinary toil is transformed into acts of hope and love. Anything we do in love makes God happy. No act is too small for love.

If, after you've considered this advice and prayed about it, you still feel your true talents are going to waste, talk to the others in your organization. Seek their advice. Pray about it. Trust that God's way will be made clear to you.

Infuse all my actions, Holy One,

no matter how small,

with hope and love.

58

The ends do not justify the means!

This applies to many areas of our lives, often in ways we overlook. For example, you are to be commended for your dedication to your neighbor's well-being—but do not let your own well-being suffer because of that dedication. Don't try to justify the harm you do your own body by thinking it's necessary in order to care for other bodies. Be careful also in all your business interactions, taking care you do not excuse underhanded financial strategies, even if they appear to benefit the work of justice.

Focus on having integrity in all aspects of your life. Set aside time regularly for self-examination. It is all too easy to wander off the path of truth—and doing so can undermine the hope others had because of us.

I know I cannot hide from you,

Beloved Friend!

But let me not hide from myself

any hypocrisy or lack of integrity

in my actions and interactions.

59

Dramatic confrontations are not always the best way to further the work of justice.

Sometimes, we cannot avoid confronting the powers that be, and when that's the case, we should speak the truth with courage. But we should not seek out confrontations for the pure love of excitement or drama, nor should we purposefully put ourselves in harm's way if it can be avoided.

As much as possible, do your work quietly, without calling attention to yourself. Don't intentionally try to bring down the wrath of people who may be dangerous to you and your work. When the situation calls for you to speak out, do so in public, where there are witnesses.

Remember also that when you get into arguments for arguments' sake, you are not furthering the work of Heaven, nor are you bringing hope to a despairing world. Instead, you may be unconsciously defending your ego, fighting for your own power. When this is the case, you undermine the very cause you claim to serve. Don't forget that all people bear within them the Divine image; they are all potential temples of the Spirit.

Give me the courage I need to speak the truth, Creator God— and the wisdom to know when and where and how to speak it.

60

If we discern our priorities, we are better able to follow through with our work.

We cannot remedy all situations or help all people. That is a simple fact—and that's why we each need to discern the particular focus God is calling us to. If we try to go in too many directions at once, we dilute our efforts.

Then, within that Divinely focused work, we must always commit ourselves to the work that is urgent versus that which is less urgent. Since we cannot do everything, we commit to projects that will have lasting rather than temporary results, projects that will physically help and spiritually encourage the most people.

Remember, it's not enough to begin the work. We also have to ensure that it endures. When our efforts are scattered across too wide an area, we're likely to exhaust our resources (both personal and organizational) to the point that we may give up. Setting priorities helps us follow through.

When I forget, remind me,

Holy Spirit—

I don't need to do all things

for all people.

I can trust you to do that.

61

Humility, flexibility, and discernment must guide our work.

It would be nice if there was a hard-and-fast rule for every challenge we encounter in this work—but there is not! We can only proceed as best we can with humility, tackling each aspect of our work from the bottom up, working in small ways as needed before we venture into more lofty projects.

To humility, we add the Spirit's flexibility. We have an open mind and a healthy imagination, allowing us to consider new ideas. We rely on the Spirit's direction.

We also take time to carefully observe and reflect on the situation. If we are still uncertain how to proceed, we should not leap to apply a solution anyway, fearful that others will doubt our leadership. Instead, we must give the circumstances the study and consideration they require.

It's tempting, Beloved Friend,

to charge forward in this cause

that means so much to me.

Remind me

that if I hurry too fast,

I may be deaf

to your Spirit's leading,

and blind to the potential suprises

you want to show me.

.

62

A lack of resources need not block the work of Heaven.

Not having the material resources we need can be both inconvenient and frustrating. But consider all that is being done around the world by people who have far less than you do. The situation that seems to hinder you may in fact be the very condition in which Divine Goodness can best work.

If your usual sources of financial support dry up, however, do not hesitate to engage in holy fundraising. In the meantime, practice patience, trusting that God will care for you and the work you do. While you wait, go without, if necessary, so that more vulnerable people can receive the care they need.

Thank you, Life-Giver,

that your Spirit's energy

does not depend on money,

nor does my hope

rely on material things.

The work of justice calls us to love all people.

We should never refuse to reach out in love to people who have power and prestige, assuming they don't need us. Divine Goodness has entrusted us to care for all people, both those who have power and those who have none, those who have many resources and those who have few.

We are all members of a single body. What benefits one part of the body is good for the body as a whole. So remember, these individuals who seem so powerful may be the very ones most in need of Divine hope. As Saint Paul says, we adapt ourselves to all people (1 Cor. 9:22).

We should not avoid these people with the excuse that they might be a bad influence. If you're worried about that, ask God to firmly grasp your vocation with Divine strength. So long as you seek the infinite goodness of the Holy One—not your own interests but those of Jesus Christ (Phil. 2:21)—your heart and soul are protected.

During your time on Earth, Jesus,

you reached out in friendship

to all people,

both the rich and the poor,

the powerful and the vulnerable.

May I be more like you.

64

Our emotions are not necessary for the work of Heaven to be accomplished.

Don't worry if you sometimes feel emotionally dry or distant from the work you're doing. Hope is not always an action. If you're *feeling* hopeless, bring it in prayer to the Giver of Life—but keep in mind that if you are *acting* in hope, determined to continue the ongoing task of bringing justice to this world, your lack of emotion will not hinder God's purposes.

Don't compare yourself to more emotional people, thinking they must be more spiritual than you are. Some people are naturally more emotional than others, but that doesn't necessarily mean they are more hopeful. In fact, sometimes our emotions can interfere with the active hope we're called to practice.

When you feel emotionally flat, keep your commitment to God's work strong and energetic, manifested in your actions. Remember, the angels are working alongside you. Even should you stumble or fail, the angels never lose hope—and neither should you.

When I feel distant, cold, bored, or discouraged, Divine Friend, remind me I have angelic helpers. Keep my commitment to your work strong, trusting you will bring me through, as you always do.

65

**Humility is not the same
as a lack of self-confidence
nor does it require us
to think poorly of ourselves.**

Regular, honest self-examination makes us aware of areas where we are weak or in error—but objective self-examination should also make us more aware of our strengths. God has gifted each of us with abilities and talents, and we are meant to claim them and use them with authority in the work of Heaven.

So don't get down on yourself! Rest assured that the people around you see your gifts, even when you can't. Above all, remember that your firm commitment to justice is more important to God than that you shine in every area.

Self-confidence is a useful Divine gift—but having it does not make you a better person any more than a lack of confidence makes you a bad person! Be patient with yourself. Remain steady in your work for your neighbor and God, even when you doubt yourself.

When I'm uncomfortable claiming my skills, Beloved One, remind me that true humility doesn't deny the abilities you've given me.

Illness need not derail the larger work.

When you are excited about the work of Heaven, it can be frustrating if you become too sick to do the work. Keep in mind, though, that Divine Goodness works through all things, including illness. As inconvenient as it seems, sickness may be the very thing you need most to grow into the person God wants you to be.

Although your physical weakness seems to limit the tasks to which you've been called, trust that God is not hindered by your temporary withdrawal from physical activity. Divine creativity continues through all circumstances. Don't lose hope!

Give me the humility, Creator,

to know you are perfectly capable

of continuing the work

with or without me.

May times of illness

expand my heart

and lead me closer to you.

67

Although God uses illness, Divine Goodness also wants us to give our bodies the care they need.

Working harder and harder, wearing yourself out, does no good, not for you, not for the people you're trying to help, and not for God. God loves your commitment, but Divinity also wants you to use common sense. This is what Saint Paul meant when he spoke of "reasonable service" (Rom. 12:1).

Neglecting your body also sets a poor example for others. Your colleagues, particularly younger ones, may think they too must work so hard that they make themselves sick as well.

Jesus, the Incarnation of Divinity, is health and hope and life. May he keep us healthy and hopeful in body, mind, and spirit.

Help me, Life-Giver,

to practice moderation

in all things, including my work.

68

Although we blame a problem on exterior circumstances, the problem may really lie inside our own hearts and minds.

When we feel restless and bored with the work, it's tempting to blame our colleagues, the workplace, or some other external circumstance. Before we complain or possibly quit, we need to examine our interior condition. We can move to another city, devote ourselves to a new organization, or insist on working with different people—but we cannot run away from ourselves. If the problem lies within us, we will carry it with us wherever we go.

So what should we do? Instead of focusing on the imperfections and failures around us, we can engage in serious self-examination. We can also seek the advice and counsel of people we respect, who may be able to see the situation more clearly than we can.

Before I complain or quit,

Light-Giver,

remind me to seek you

within my own heart

so that I can see myself

more clearly.

69

Practice simplicity.

We tend to think some things are necessities when they are actually superfluous. We may excuse such luxuries, saying God wants us to give ourselves adequate care and comfort.

Or we may justify our extravagance by pointing to colleagues or friends whose lifestyles look just as luxurious. However, we may not have the entire picture; it may be that their well-being, for whatever reason, truly requires these extra comforts. In any case, it's none of our business!

In a world where so many people lack even basic necessities, Divine Goodness calls us to a simple lifestyle. There is no hard-and-fast rule for everyone, though. We must each discern for ourselves what simplicity means in our own lives, so that we can be light-beings reflecting the Light of Life.

Lead me, Giver of Life,

on simple paths.

70

Divine Goodness calls us to demonstrate love to all people, regardless of their ethnic background or nationality.

We cannot do the work of Heaven if we show favoritism to one group of people over another. Human beings naturally feel closer to some people than others, but when it comes to justice, we cannot let these feelings influence us.

With regular self-examination, we can identify the prejudices we hide even from ourselves.

Get my attention, Just One,
when you see any form of prejudice
influencing my interactions.
May I never be so sure of myself
that I refuse to examine
my motivations.
Remind me I am not immune to
the very things I criticize in others—
and that discrimination
and intolerance
are the enemies of hope.

We each have our own role to play in the work of Heaven.

In the human body, we have many organs. Though each is necessary to the well-being of the entire body, we could not function if we were all eyes or ears or hands or feet. Each organ has its own role to play, and each body part's work is the exercise of its unique abilities.

The same is true for us as we do the work of Heaven. Rather than envying other people's abilities or position, we are each called to make use of our own skills in the place where they are most useful to the work.

Help me, All-Maker,

not to seek out new roles

simply because they're showier

or look more exciting.

May I instead, with all my heart,

do the work I do best,

so that my actions spread hope,

even in the smallest of ways.

72

Exploitive sexual indulgence puts our work at risk.

Few human beings are immune from sexual temptation, but if we yield to this attractive lure, engaging in exploitative sexual practices, we can harm or even undo the work we seek to accomplish.

If we face this temptation, we are not helpless. We can counter it with prayer. Practice seeing Jesus in all people. Instead of seeing individuals as sexual objects, recognize that each one is the image of the Trinity. Another practical tactic is to avoid spending much time alone with either colleagues or clients. Maintain your own boundaries, and don't encourage people to cross them. Notice the occasions and circumstances where you feel most tempted—and avoid them!

Most of all, focus on living in the Divine Presence. Remember that Infinite Wisdom is both within you and all around you.

May my sexuality

praise you, Life-Giver.

Pride says we have to be perfect in all things; humility accepts that we're not.

Self-examination is healthy and essential to both your spiritual life and your exterior work—but don't become too preoccupied with your various faults and mistakes. This preoccupation is actually the opposite of true humility, for it encourages you to focus on yourself rather than on others. If you're constantly worried you might make a mistake, you become frozen, hopeless, unable to do the work God wants you to do.

If you find yourself in this dilemma, seek help from a trusted counselor or friend who will see things more objectively. Talk to God about it. Do not be embarrassed to ask others to pray for you.

Thank you, Beloved Friend,

that you know me inside and out.

I trust you with both my skills

and my weaknesses.

Give me the courage I need

to also trust your servants,

the beings who share my life,

so that their insight

might help me see

your Light.

74

God gives us the exact portion of time we truly need.

When there's just not enough time in the day for all your work, ask Jesus to help you. Examine the hours to see what is actually taking up so much of your time: Is there anything relatively unimportant you could spend less time on so that you'd have time for more important tasks? As always, engage in prayerful self-examination.

The busier you are, the more vital it is that you set aside a little time for yourself. Far from interfering with your work, this time will actually make you more effective. It will allow you to find greater clarity as to how your time can be used most efficiently.

May I never, Infinite Goodness,

be too busy for you.

We need recreation—and God blesses the world through our pleasure.

In our eagerness to serve God and the world, we sometimes think any activity that gives us pleasure must be a waste of time. Our passionate commitment to God's work may cause us to practice such stringent self-discipline that we deny our bodies the rest and exercise they need. Even if our work does not demand much physical effort, unrelenting mental effort can also wear us down. It's hard to feel hopeful when we're exhausted.

How can we be of any use to the work of Heaven if our minds and bodies are weary and weak? God created our bodies with their needs, and Divinity wants us to experience well-being in both our souls and our bodies.

Thank you, Creator,

for time off from work.

76

Opposition to our work can make it even stronger.

Don't be discouraged if people condemn and harass your work. Even if they use scripture to back up their actions, stay true to your calling. Don't let them rob you of your hope. Have confidence in God's guidance.

Very often, the efforts that face the most opposition are the ones that prove to have the most effect. Challenges such as these will allow your work to build a strong foundation, so that it can grow strong for years to come.

May God make it so!

When people

give me a hard time, Eternal One,

may I stay true to you

and to the hope to which

you have called me (Eph. 1:18).

THE EXAMEN

The Examen is a prayer tool Ignatius devised to keep our self-awareness steady, despite all that life throws at us. It can be adapted to life's various demands, but it generally follows this basic outline:

1. Place yourself in God's presence, thanking God for the love that surrounds you.

2. Pray for insight into the ways God is acting in your life. This insight will generate hope.

3. Review the past day, recalling specific moments and your emotional reactions.

4. Reflect on what you did, said, or thought on each of those occasions. Did you feel closer to God—or further away?

5. Look toward the future, thinking about how you might collaborate more deeply with Divine hope for your life and the world around you.

Ignatius created a daily "anchor"
that will hold you steady,
even in the midst of a turbulent world.

NOTES

1. In 1542, Ignatius wrote to eighty young Jesuit students after he learned that their excessive fervor was leading them to discipline themselves in the city streets, preach half-clothed, and shout out cries of penitence in the middle of the night, waking their neighbors. Ignatius praises the students and affirms all they are doing well before he criticizes them. Meditations 1-13 are drawn from this letter.

14. Ignatius wrote this advice in December 1553, to encourage a rector at the college in Modena.

15. This meditation is based on a letter, written sometime in 1543, that was directed to a man called Bobadilla. As a Jesuit, he was a tireless worker who served God in Germany, Italy, and Dalmatia until his death at 81.

16. Written in December 1545, this counsel sprang from Ignatius's concern for a Capuchin priest who was in trouble with the Vatican for preaching Protestant theology. Ignatius wanted the Jesuits to do all they could to help this man, acting in the love of Christ.

17. Written in December 1542, the original letter addressed the lively exchange of written communications between the Jesuits.

Long before text messaging and emailing, these well-educated men were dashing off letters with little concern for the contents. Ignatius was all too aware that anything put in writing can have a powerful effect, for good and ill, especially when it falls into the hands of people other than those for whom it was intended.

18. In January 1551, Ignatius, after reflection and self-examination, felt he should resign as the Society's general. The Jesuits' Constitutions were completed, Ignatius was getting older, and he thought someone else might now do the job better than he could. This meditation is based on the letter he wrote expressing these thoughts. The elder fathers in Rome disagreed, and with humility, Ignatius accepted their decision as God's way for his life and for the Jesuits. He remained general until his death 5 years later.

19. Meditations 19 and 20 are drawn from the same letter. In June of 1592, Ignatius heard that the pope had recommended that Francis Borgia become a bishop. Ignatius disagreed with this course of action (as did Francis, apparently), while other Jesuits were enthusiastic about the possibility. Ignatius describes the process of discernment he underwent. Ultimately, Francis Borgia became the third Superior General of the Society of Jesus, but he was never ordained a bishop.

21. Meditations 21–31 are drawn from the same document, written in 1543. Ignatius sent these instructions to students at Alcalá as guidelines for spiritual growth.

32. In 1541, the pope sent a group of Jesuits to Ireland, hoping they would rekindle the Catholic faith in a land that was turning toward Protestantism. The Jesuits were not welcomed, and

after a little more than a month, they gave up and went home. Meditations 32–37 are drawn from Ignatius's instructions to the delegates during their time in an unfriendly environment.

38. In 1542, the pope and King John III of Portugal were locked in a power conflict. Ignatius felt caught in the middle. This meditation is based on a letter he wrote to the Jesuit ambassador to Portugal, hoping to encourage him to bring about a peaceful reconciliation between the king and the pope.

39. Pope Paul III asked Ignatius for three Jesuits to serve as theologians at the Council of Trent; Ignatius appointed Diego Laínez, Alfonso Salmerón, and Pierre Favre. Meditations 39–42 are drawn from his advice to the delegates, written in 1546.

43. Meditations 43–47 are inspired by a letter Ignatius wrote to Francisco de Borja in 1548 after Borja had asked for advice regarding the spiritual disciplines he was practicing. In response, Ignatius basically told him to lighten up! Ignatius had learned from experience that extreme asceticism did not make him more spiritual; it only weakened his body and made him ill.

48. In early 1549, Wilhelm IV, Duke of Bavaria, sent a request to Pope Paul III for three Jesuits to teach at the University of Ingolstadt. Meditations 48–50 are drawn from Ignatius's letter of advice to the three men.

51. In 1551, Ignatius, via his secretary, sent his advice on the spiritual life to a group of Jesuits in Portugal. Meditations 51–52 are drawn from that letter.

53. This meditation is inspired by a letter Ignatius wrote in June 1551 to a family connection who was also a Jesuit working in Spain. Ignatius had received word that the other man was not

eating properly, could not sleep, and was so weak that his physician had ordered him to take some time off from his work in order to recuperate.

54. Ignatius assigned three of his followers to the Jesuit college in Ferrara, which opened in 1551. He then sent them a letter filled with practical instructions for their work. Meditations 54–56 are based on this letter.

57. When Manuel Godinho was appointed in 1552 to be treasurer of the college in Coimbra, he was uncomfortable with the "worldly" and financial responsibilities his new position required. Godinho was accustomed to an austere and ascetic lifestyle, and he felt his new work was interfering with his spiritual life. This meditation is drawn from Ignatius's response to Godinho's complaints.

58. As the Society grew in membership, Ignatius sent Jesuits to other countries around the world, as well as to the major European cities. In October 1552, Ignatius jotted down the principles that ought to guide the Jesuits in their ministries. Meditations 58–61 are based on this letter.

62. This meditation is inspired by a letter Ignatius wrote to his followers on Christmas Eve 1552.

63. In July 1552, John III of Portugal asked the new provincial, Diego Miró, to give him spiritual direction. Miró made a long string of excuses, among them that the king did not know him, that he was a foreigner, and that it was more fitting for Jesuits to work among vulnerable people rather than the powerful. This meditation comes from Ignatius's response to the situation.

64. Nicholas Goudanus, a Jesuit working in Germany and Austria, wrote to Ignatius to ask for prayer that he might receive the "gift of tears." Apparently, he was feeling emotionally dry. This meditation, written in November 1553, is based on Ignatius's response.

65. In 1553, when Philip Leernus was appointed to be rector of the college at Modena, he wrote to Ignatius, protesting that he wasn't equipped to do the job well. This meditation is drawn from Ignatius's answer

66. This meditation comes from a letter Ignatius wrote in January 1554 to a disobedient Jesuit who had fallen ill.

67. Gaspar Berze, a Jesuit missionary in India, had worn himself out by working too hard. This meditation, written in 1554, is drawn from Ignatius's advice to Berze. Unfortunately, by the time the letter reached India, Berze was already dead.

68. A Jesuit named Bartolomeo, who was serving at the college in Ferrara, was discontented and restless, full of complaints about the school and his colleagues. This meditation comes from the advice Ignatius sent to him in January 1555.

69. This meditation is drawn from a letter Ignatius sent in May 1556 to the rector at the college in Louvain.

70. This meditation is based on a letter Ignatius wrote in May 1556 to Lorenzo of Modeno.

71. This counsel is based on a letter Ignatius sent in May 1556 to Giovanni Battisti who was hoping to change his job within the Society of Jesus.

72. Ignatius wrote his original letter in May 1556 to Emerio de Bonis, a Jesuit teacher in Padua, who was having problems with sexual temptation.

73. Juan Marín, a young Jesuit teaching at the college in Bivona, Sicily, was good at his work and showed great promise. He was plagued, however, by what was called "scruples"—an over-active conscience that drove him to focus too much on his imperfections. Ignatius was especially interested in him, since he too, in his early years, had suffered from scruples. This meditation comes from the letter he wrote Marin in June 1556.

74. This advice is drawn from a letter Ignatius wrote in July 1556.

75. Ignatius's counsel here is drawn from a letter he wrote to a Jesuit teacher in Tivoli in July 1556.

76. Father Román, the rector of the Jesuit community in Saragossa, wrote to Ignatius to tell him of the difficulties the community was facing: "opposition and whispering campaigns, false reports, jealousy, jeering, and mockery." Anti-Jesuit posters were pasted around the city, including on the walls of the Jesuit chapel, and anti-Jesuit demonstrations took place, during which the Jesuits' windows were broken as people chanted and sang songs, claiming scriptural authority for their actions. This meditation is drawn from a short letter Ignatius wrote in 1556, two weeks before he died.

The Spiritual Work of Racial Justice
A Month of Meditations with Ignatius of Loyola

"*The Spiritual Work of Racial Justice* is a meaningful and practical resource for our times. Through Ignatian Spiritual Exercises, Patrick Saint-Jean, S.J. offers an opportunity to continue the pursuit of racial justice as a necessary component of faith. Each meditation includes relevant history and grounded spiritual practices. The book is refreshing and accessible to all."

— Barbara Holmes, author of *Joy Unspeakable: Contemplative Practices of the Black Church* and *Liberation and the Cosmos*

"Saint-Jean's book beautifully weaves together several threads: the author's personal experience as a Jesuit in formation who is both an immigrant and a Black man; poignant reminders of the long history of race-based violence; calls for racial justice; and the perennial wisdom of the Spiritual Exercises of St. Ignatius of Loyola, with their focus on examining our sin so that we are free to love God and neighbor. The end result is an invitation to the interior work necessary to deepen our commitment to racial justice."

— Very Rev. Brian G. Paulson, S.J., Provincial Superior, USA Midwest Province of the Society of Jesus

Persistent Resistance
Calls for Justice from the Celtic Traditions
A Collection of Essays

The Celts were activists for justice. They persuaded kings to change their policies; they stood up for women and others who were endangered by prejudice; and they worked with tireless love on behalf of all Earth's creatures. They resisted the injustice of their day—and they persisted throughout their entire lifetimes, until their deaths. (And some would say that they are still hard at work fighting injustice from the Otherworld.) Following in their footsteps requires a mystical experience of the Divine that expresses itself in acts of tangible justice and compassion

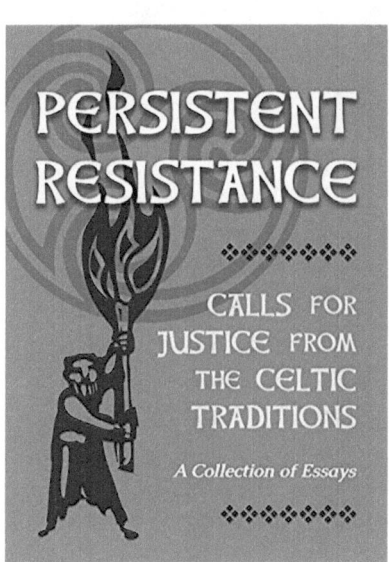

These essays build on Celtic stories, myths, and tradition to inspire and challenge us. They remind us that we cannot consider ourselves faithful to God if we are not faithful to our entire community (a community that not only includes humans, but also animals, plants, and the entire Earth).

Paths of Justice
Celtic Prayers for a World of Equity, Unity, and Healing

Energize us with Your compassion, Giver of Life, to help the dispossessed, to listen to those without voices, and to reach out in friendship to all. Empower us with Your love; encourage us with Your Spirit; make us strong to bring Your justice to individuals, communities, nations, and the entire globe.

Our society often assumes that "justice" has to do with punishment. We think it means we make criminals pay for their crimes. The biblical meaning of the word "justice," however, means "to make right." This concept of justice has to do

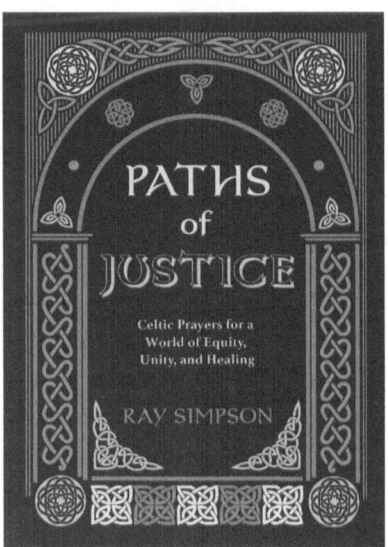

with healthy relationships based on equity and kindness; it refers to a society based on life-giving relationships between God, human beings, and the natural world. This is the world Ray Simpson seeks to build, and he offers these prayers as openings into the Divine power that constantly seeks to heal and restore.

101 Soul Seeds
for Peacemakers & Justice-Seekers

Authentic spirituality embeds us in the pain of the world and inspires commitment to social justice and conflict resolution. It seeks peace and justice in the public sphere, while nurturing a sense of connection with both God and all creation. Rooted in the deep mystery of Divine love, we can face challenges with confidence that God's vision of justice and peace will outlast the demagogues, dictators, and destroyers.

This book is intended to support your integration of peacemaking, justice-seeking, and spiritual growth.

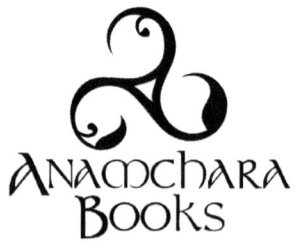

AnamcharaBooks.com

www.ingramcontent.com/pod-product-compliance
Lightning Source LLC
Chambersburg PA
CBHW060524080526
44586CB00012B/602